Paper Airplanes
and
Other Super Flyers

Written by Neil Francis

Illustrations by June Bradford

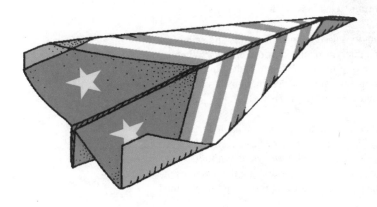

KIDS CAN PRESS LTD.

TORONTO

Kids Can Press Ltd. acknowledges with appreciation the
assistance of the Canada Council and the Ontario Arts Council
in the production of this book.

Canadian Cataloguing in Publication Data

Francis, Neil
    Paper airplanes and other super flyers

Rev. ed.
First ed. published under title: Super flyers.

ISBN 1-55074-328-7 (bound)   ISBN 1-55074-307-4 (pbk.)

1. Paper airplanes — Juvenile literature. 2. Aeronautics —
Juvenile literature. I. Bradford, June. II. Title.

TL770.F73 1996   j745.592   C96-930055-7

This edition of *Paper Airplanes and Other Super Flyers* has been
produced exclusively for Irwin Toys, 43 Hanna Avenue,
Toronto, ON, Canada, M6K 1X6.

Kids Can Press Ltd.
29 Birch Avenue
Toronto, Ontario, Canada
M4V 1E2

Edited by Elizabeth MacLeod
Designed by Karen Powers
Art colourized by First Folio Resource Group, Inc.
Printed in Hong Kong

96 0 9 8 7 6 5 4 3 2 1

Contents

Chapter One

GLIDERS

The gliders you'll make in this chapter are all fixed-wing gliders. Like birds gliding with their wings extended, these gliders have fixed, not flapping, wings. They also have controls to help them fly — and do some pretty amazing aerobatics. And if you decorate these gliders with stickers or markers and colored pencils, they'll look great as they perform.

Dart

The Dart starts out as a traditional paper airplane and then gets spiced up with flying controls that are the same as the controls on a real airplane.

YOU WILL NEED

- a piece of paper 22 cm x 28 cm (8½ in. x 11 in.)
- clear tape, scissors, a ruler

1 Fold the paper in half the long way, then open it.

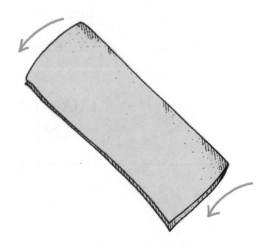

2 Fold the two corners in to the center fold line.

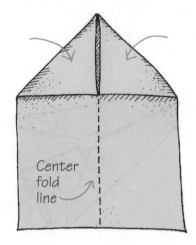

Center fold line

5 Fold one side out and down to meet the center fold line. Do the same with the other side.

Side view

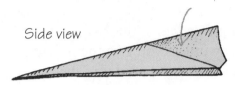

Other side view

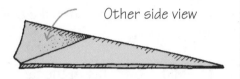

3 Fold corners A in to the center fold line.

A 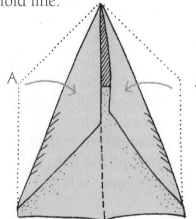 A

6 Swing the wings up into a horizontal position. The Dart should come to a sharp point in front.

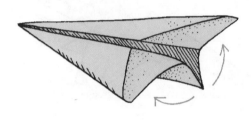

4 Fold over and crease.

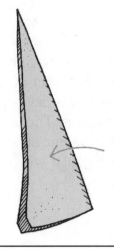

7 Tape the sides together as shown.

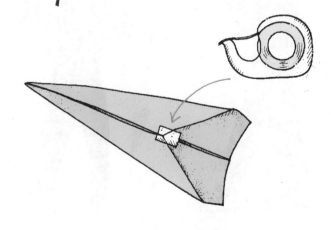

Finishing the Dart

THE ELEVATORS

Many of the gliders in this book will be nose-heavy unless you give them flying controls to bring the nose up. The control that moves the nose of an airplane up or down is called the elevator. Here's how to make elevators for your Dart.

1 Make four cuts in the tail of your glider as shown. Each should be about 1 cm (½ in.) long. The flaps between the cuts are the elevators.

2 Bend the elevators up. The farther up the elevators are bent, the harder they will pull the nose up. Bend the elevators up only a little at first.

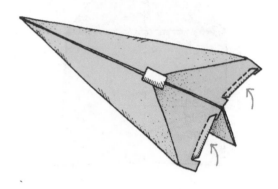

3 Test-fly the Dart to find the correct angle for the elevators. If it still nosedives, bend the elevators up more. If it swoops and falls, reduce the angle slightly.

As you can see, the Dart has a triangular-shaped wing. That's a wing shape that rarely if ever occurs in nature — it was developed by humans. The Concorde supersonic airliner has triangular wings.

THE RUDDER

The control that moves the plane right or left is the rudder. Here's how to make a rudder for your Dart.

1 Make a cut about 1 cm (½ in.) long on the vertical fin at the back of your glider.

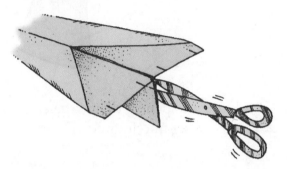

2 To make the Dart turn to the left, bend the rudder a bit to the left.

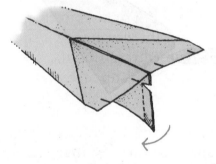

3 To make the glider turn to the right, bend the rudder to the right. The more the rudder is bent, the sharper the glider will turn. Also, the more the rudder is bent, the more steeply the Dart dives. For tight turns it may be necessary to bend the elevators up to keep the glider from diving too steeply.

THE AILERONS

The controls that make the Dart roll over one way or the other are called the ailerons. Because this glider stays level when it flies, you don't need ailerons. However, if you want your Dart to do a roll, you can make the elevators behave like ailerons. Here's how:

1 Bend one elevator up and the other down.

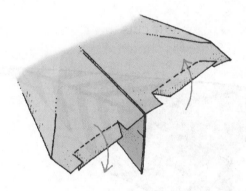

2 Give your Dart a hard throw. The glider will roll in the direction of the elevator that is up.

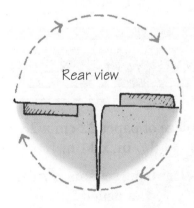

Rear view

Starship

This glider has turned-up wing tips, called winglets. These are also used on some real airplanes.

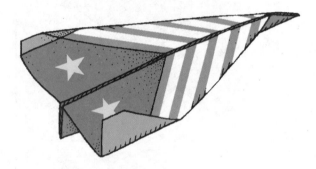

YOU WILL NEED

- a piece of paper 22 cm x 28 cm (8½ in. x 11 in.)
- clear tape, scissors, a ruler, a pencil

1 Proceed as you did for the Dart but stop after step 4. Your glider should look like this:

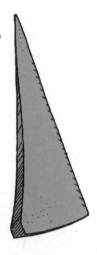

2 Using the pencil, divide the end of each wing into four equal parts.

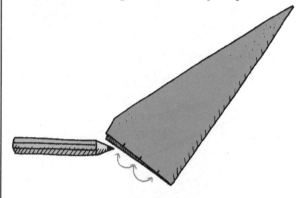

3 On one wing, make a fold at the pencil mark nearest to the center fold. The fold is parallel to the center fold, as shown.

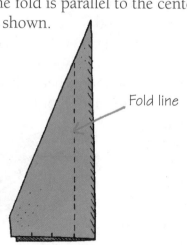

Fold line

4 Fold the wing down along the fold line.

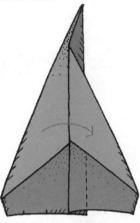

5 Do the same with the other wing.

6 The side view should look like this. Fold the tips of each wing back. This fold should start about 2 cm (¾ in.) from the wing tip. These are your winglets.

7 Swing the wings up and the winglets out as shown. Before flying the Starship, follow the finishing instructions on pages 6 to 7.

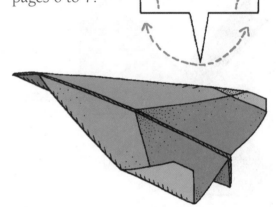

Other Ideas

The Dart and the Starship fly well outdoors. If the wind blows your glider around too much, add some weight by attaching one or two paper clips to the bottom, about halfway between the nose and tail.

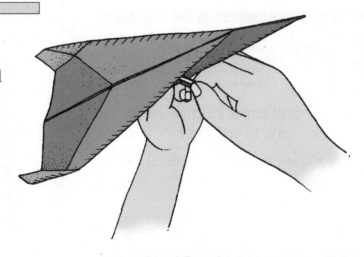

Origami Aerobat

This is one of the world's best paper airplane designs. The type of paper folding used to make it was invented in Japan and is called origami.

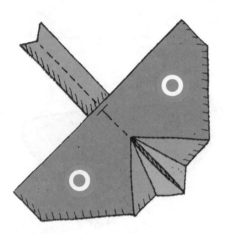

YOU WILL NEED

- a piece of paper 22 cm x 28 cm (8½ in. x 11 in.)

- scissors, a ruler, a pencil

1 Cut a strip of paper 5 cm (2 in.) wide from the top of the paper. This will be your Aerobat's tail.

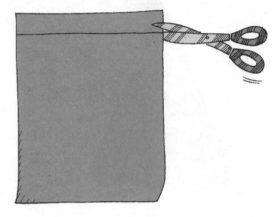

2 Make a crease down the center of the tail, and fold the ends up as shown. Set the tail aside.

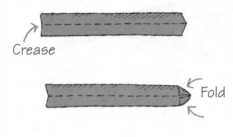

Crease

Fold

3 Mark B for bottom and T for top on your paper.

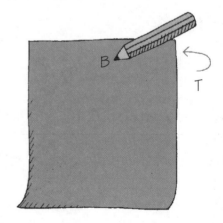

B

T

4 With B at the top, fold one edge over to meet the other edge, then open so that you can see the crease. Do the same with the other edge.

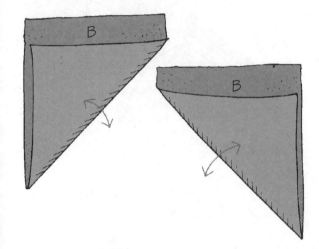

6 Turn the paper over so that T is up, and fold as shown. Unfold to leave a crease.

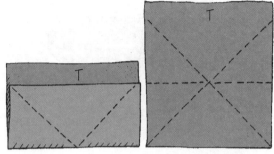

7 Turn the paper over again so that B is up. Bend the two sides in as shown and press flat.

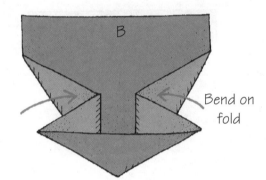

Bend on fold

5 When you open the paper, it should have creases that look like this:

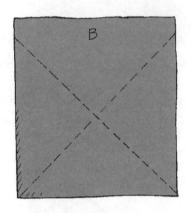

8 Fold as shown.

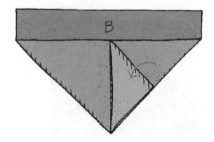

9 Fold as shown, then open to leave a crease.

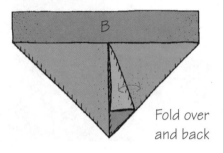

Fold over and back

10 Fold as shown, then open to leave a crease.

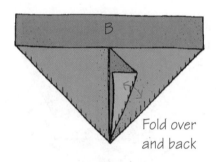

Fold over and back

11 You should now have creases that cross like this:

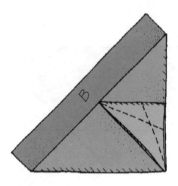

12 Fold in the crease lines and pinch up the center as shown, then ...

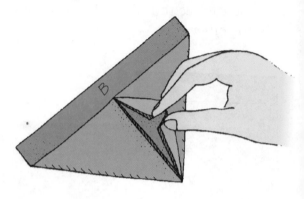

13 ... fold the pinched-up portion toward the nose.

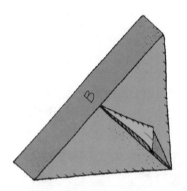

14 Repeat steps 8 to 13 on the other side. Your Aerobat should look like this when you're done:

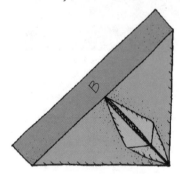

15 Fold the nose point under, along the line indicated by the dots.

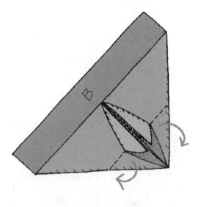

16 Your Aerobat should look like this:

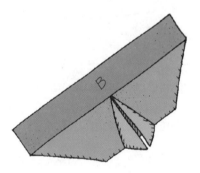

17 Fold the plane in half to make a crease.

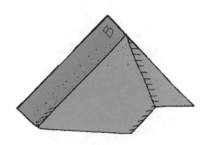

18 Unfold the plane and pull the rest of the nose up again.

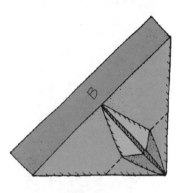

19 Insert the tail as shown.

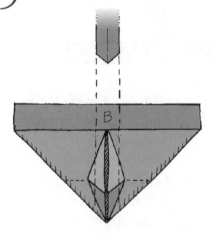

20 Fold the nose down again, leaving the split nose up.

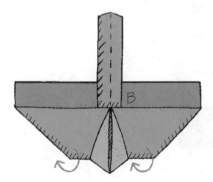

Finishing the Aerobat

1 Turn the Aerobat over so that T is up, then fold the Aerobat along the center crease so that the wings are bent up slightly.

4 You can also try making a gull-wing fold. To do this, fold up on the center crease and out on the outer fold lines.

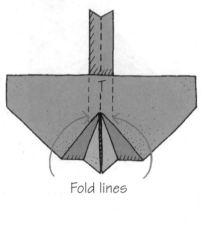

Fold lines

End view

2 Throw the Aerobat gently. It should glide straight ahead or turn slightly to one side.

3 If the Aerobat does tight turns or spins down, make sure it isn't wrinkled or bent out of shape, then bend the wings up more.

5 If your Aerobat still doesn't fly well, try bending down the wing tips or making a new Aerobat.

Tips bent down

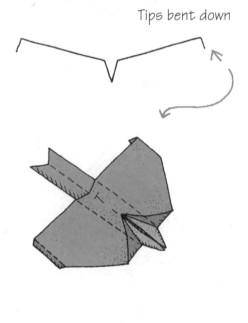

Aerobat Aerobatics

Fly the Aerobat by holding it between your thumb and forefinger and throwing it gently. Once you've got the hang of flying it, try these aerobatics.

THE LOOP
Throw hard.

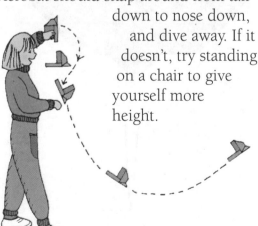

THE TAIL TOSS
Hold the Aerobat as shown and throw it tail first, as if it were a ball. The Aerobat will flip around as it leaves your hand and may do some exciting aerobatics. The tail toss takes some practice but results in higher, longer flights.

THE FLICK ROLL
Hold the Aerobat by one wing and throw it as you would a Frisbee.

THE TAIL SLIDE
Hold the Aerobat nose up with the tail pointing straight down. Drop it. The Aerobat should snap around from tail down to nose down, and dive away. If it doesn't, try standing on a chair to give yourself more height.

Origami Twin Tail

This speedy twin-tailed origami glider is based on the Origami Aerobat.

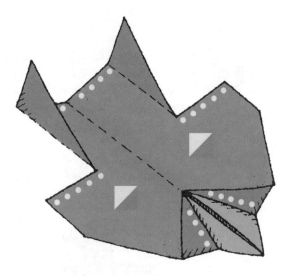

1 Follow steps 3 to 16 for the Origami Aerobat on pages 10 to 13.

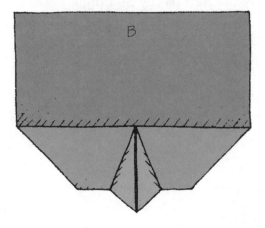

2 Turn the glider over so that T is up. Bend the wings up so they touch.

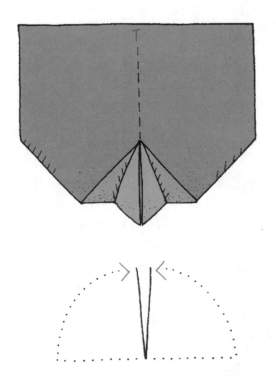

3 Hold the wings together and make two cuts as shown.

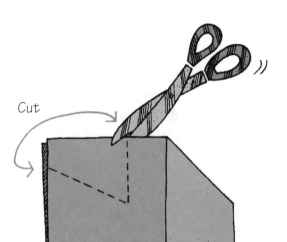

Cut

5 Finish the Origami Twin Tail by bending this wing up more. For help on how to do this, see page 14.

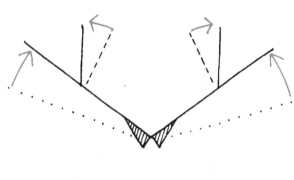

4 Open the wings. Fold the edges of the tail up along the fold lines as shown. These are your plane's rudders.

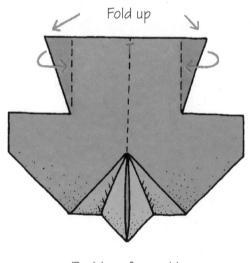

Fold up

Rudders formed by folded-up tail

6 Make sure the rudders are always straight up and down, not bent at an angle. Fly the Twin Tail the same way you flew the Origami Aerobat (see page 15).

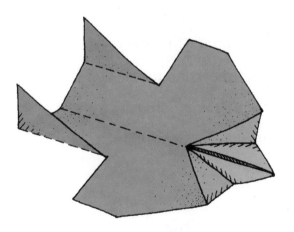

Chapter Two

TWIRLING WINGS

The idea of a twirling or turning wing, instead of a fixed wing, has been around for a long time. Watch a maple tree seed spinning down from a tree and you will see that it quickly gets where it's going by twirling through the air. The twirling-wing flyers in this chapter are also terrific flyers — and they're easy to make. If you like, decorate them using stickers or markers and paints.

Dirigible

This is probably the easiest flying machine to make in the whole book. It does a steep glide and rotates furiously as it falls.

YOU WILL NEED

- a strip of paper 2 cm x 21 cm
  (¾ in. x 8¼ in.)
- scissors

1 Make a cut at each end of the paper strip as shown. Be sure that each cut goes only halfway across the paper and that the cuts are on opposite sides.

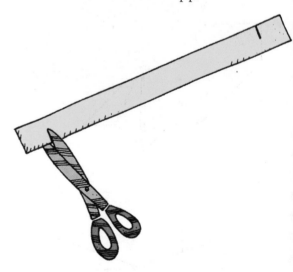

2 Bend the paper (do not fold it) so that the two cuts fit into each other.

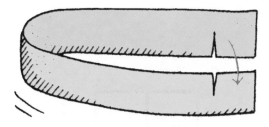
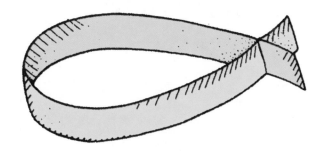

3 To fly the Dirigible, hold it above your head and drop it. As it falls, it will start spinning and look like a dirigible. The spinning makes it stable in the air. Try flying your Dirigible from somewhere high — from the top of some stairs, for instance.

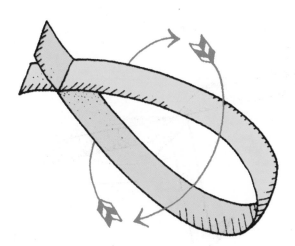

Other Ideas

How big a dirigible can you make and fly? How small?

A real dirigible has a rigid framework that is covered in cloth. Gas bags inside the framework make it float in the air. A dirigible is moved through the air by engines and propellers that are controlled by a pilot. The pilot sits in a cabin called a control gondola.

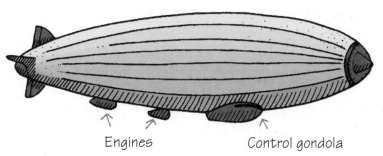

Engines   Control gondola

Rotoglide

*Round and round and down — the
Rotoglide will sail with its wings twirling
around like a helicopter rotor blade.*

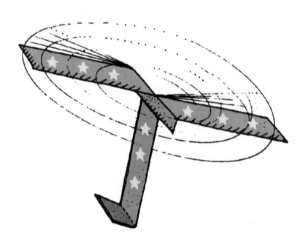

YOU WILL NEED

- a piece of paper 25 cm x 6 cm
  (10 in. x 2¼ in.)

- scissors, a ruler, a pencil

1 Mark your paper with solid lines
and dotted lines as shown. Cut
along the solid lines.

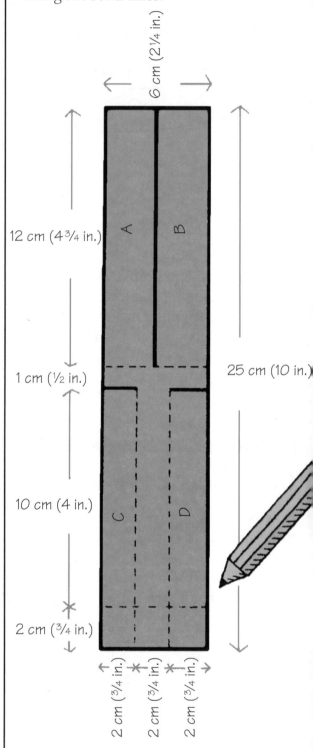

6 cm (2¼ in.)

12 cm (4¾ in.)

1 cm (½ in.)

10 cm (4 in.)

2 cm (¾ in.)

25 cm (10 in.)

A

B

C

D

2 cm (¾ in.)   2 cm (¾ in.)   2 cm (¾ in.)

2 Fold A and B in opposite directions.

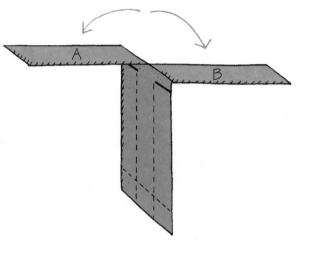

3 Fold C and D toward each other so that they overlap.

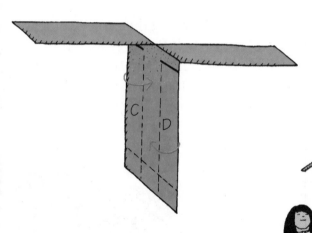

4 Fold the bottom up.

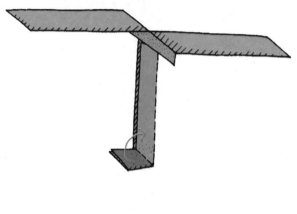

5 To fly the Rotoglide, hold it over your head and drop it. It will glide to the floor spinning. The higher you start your Rotoglide's flight, the farther it will go.

If your Rotoglide wobbles, add a paper clip or other small weight to the bottom.

Heliostraw

*This rotary glider doesn't just glide —
it can also climb and hover.*

YOU WILL NEED

- a strip of cardboard 2 cm x 21 cm
  (¾ in. x 8¼ in.)

- masking tape

- a plastic drinking straw

- scissors, a ruler, a pencil,
a one-hole punch (optional)

1 To find the center point of the
wing, draw two lines on your piece
of cardboard from corner to corner.

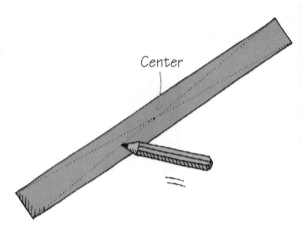

Center

2 Make a hole at the center point
that is slightly bigger than the
width (diameter) of the straw. Use the
hole punch or the point of the scissors
to make this hole.

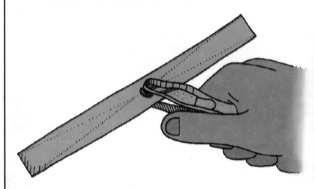

3 Make cuts 1 cm (½ in.) long on each side of the hole as shown. Fold the wing in half lengthwise and unfold it.

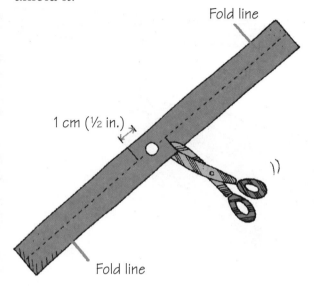

Fold line

1 cm (½ in.)

Fold line

4 Wrap tape around one end of the straw so that the wrapped end fits snugly into the hole in the wing. If the wing wobbles, tape the straw to the wing to hold it firm.

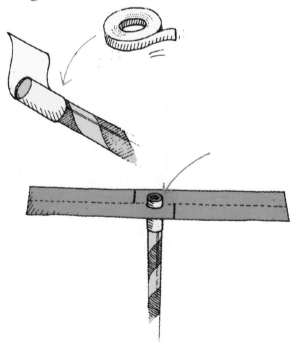

5 Fold under the last 1 cm (½ in.) of the wing tips. Tape these folds down. This will add weight to the wing tips and increase momentum as the wing spins.

1 cm (½ in.)

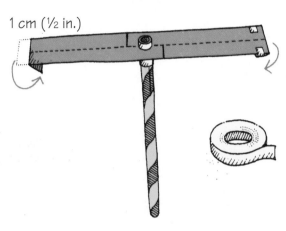

6 From the cuts outward, bend the edges of the wing down slightly along the fold line, as shown. Do not bend the edges down too much — they should just gently curve. Make sure both edges of the wing are bent down the same amount.

Bend down

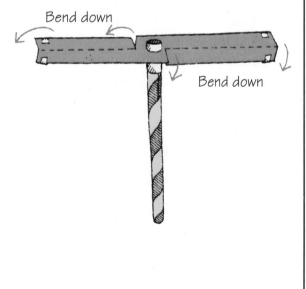

Bend down

7 To fly the Heliostraw, hold the straw between your palms. Roll your palms together so that the wing rotates rapidly counterclockwise. Let go. The Heliostraw will spin out of your hand.

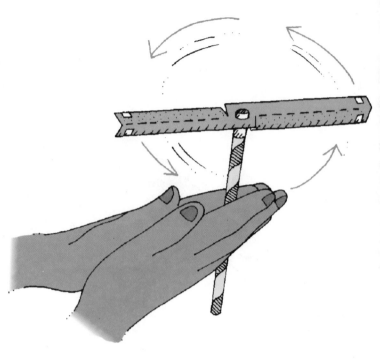

8 If the wing spins but the Heliostraw won't climb, bend the edges of the wing down more. If the Heliostraw climbs rapidly but stops spinning almost immediately, try reducing the amount of bend at the wing edges. Experiment to find the wing setting that works best for you.

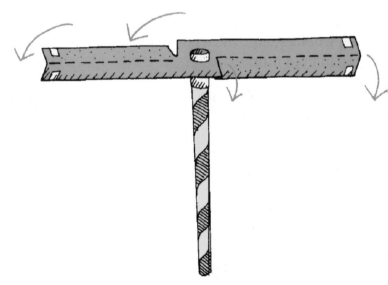

Heliostraw Aerobatics

THE GLIDE
Spin the Heliostraw gently backward (clockwise) and let it go. It will spin down just like the Rotoglide.

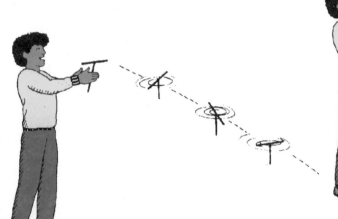

Holding the straw straight up and down, spin the Heliostraw gently counter-clockwise and let it go. It should climb and hover before gliding down.

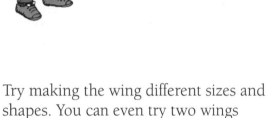

Try making the wing different sizes and shapes. You can even try two wings instead of one.

FAST FORWARD
Tilt the straw away from you and fly it.

Chapter Three

WHAT IS IT?

In the world of flying and airplanes, there are always a few what-is-its around. What-is-its are super flyers that don't look like anything else. Some have circular wings, others have no wings at all, while still others are made out of materials that may surprise you! Have fun decorating these what-is-its with markers, paints or stickers.

Straw Glider

The Straw Glider has round, or circular, wings. Circular wings have been tried on real airplanes almost since the beginning of aviation, but they have never been very successful. On the Straw Glider they work very well.

YOU WILL NEED

- two strips of paper,
one 2 cm x 16 cm (¾ in. x 6¼ in.)
and the other 1.5 cm x 14 cm
(⅝ in. x 5½ in.)

- a plastic drinking straw 21 cm
(8¼ in.) long

- clear tape

1 Bend the large strip of paper into a circle so that the ends overlap slightly. Tape the two places shown. The overlap will form a pocket into which the straw will fit.

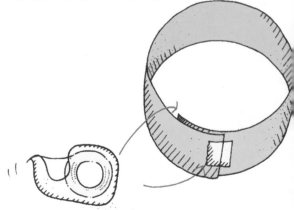

2 Pry open the pocket and slip it over one end of the straw.

3 Bend the smaller strip of paper into a circle and tape it as in step 1. Slip it over the other end of the straw.

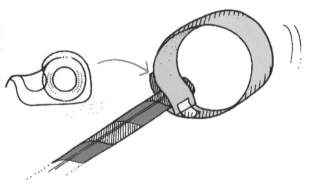

4 Move the two paper circles (the circular wings) until they are both positioned above the straw as shown. Tape them in place.

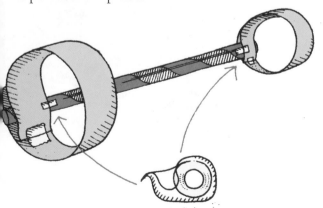

5 Looking down on the glider, make sure that the wings are at right angles to the straw. If they're not, loosen the tape and retape the wings so they are straight.

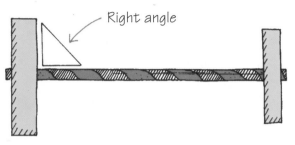

Right angle

6 To fly the Straw Glider, hold it by the straw with the smaller wing to the front and throw gently.

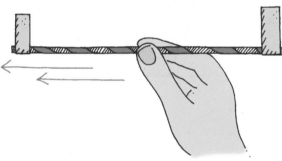

Flying Tips

If the Straw Glider nosedives, move the large wing forward slightly and try again. If you move it too far forward, the glider will wobble through the air.

If the Straw Glider wobbles when you first fly it, move the small wing back slightly and try again. Properly adjusted, the glider should have a long, flat glide.

Twirl-o-Tube

Lightweight tubes can fly if a few adjustments are made to them. The secret is to add weight to the front to make the tube spin or rotate while in the air.

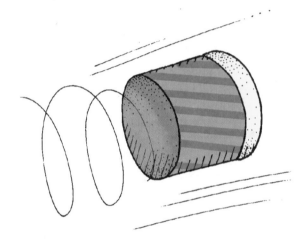

- the cardboard tube from a roll of paper towels or bathroom tissue
- heavy tape such as masking tape
- scissors, a ruler

1 Measure the distance across the end of the tube. This is called the diameter. Cut the tube so that it is the same length as or just a bit longer than the diameter. This tube has a diameter of 4 cm (1 ½ in.), so it is cut 4 cm (1 ½ in.) long.

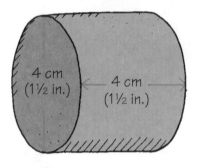

4 cm (1½ in.)   4 cm (1½ in.)

2 Wrap a layer of heavy tape around one end as shown.

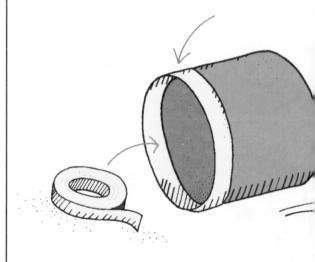

3 Throw the tube so that it goes tape end forward and rotates at the same time. To do this, try an underhand throw. Let the tube roll off your fingers as you throw to give it a spin. You can adjust the tube to make it fly better, but be sure to perfect your throwing technique first.

4 If the Twirl-o-Tube wobbles as it flies, add another layer of tape to the nose and try again. Keep adding tape to the nose until the wobble is almost gone.

If the tube gets too heavy and will not glide far, take off some of the tape. You might not be able to eliminate the wobble completely because the paper tube may be a little too heavy to begin with.

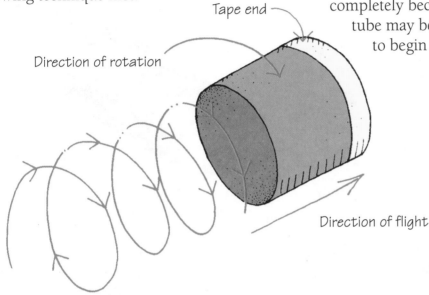

Tape end

Direction of rotation

Direction of flight

How It Works

Twirl-o-Tubes are circular flying wings without bodies, or fuselages. Airplane designers know that a flying wing by itself makes a very efficient airplane; it doesn't have a fuselage to weigh it down. But there are two reasons why no really successful full-sized flying wing has been built. First, with no fuselage, there's no room for cargo, baggage or even a crew. Second, there are problems with stability.

Your Twirl-o-Tube doesn't have stability problems, because it spins as it flies.

Spinning makes things stable — just think of a spinning top. When a circular object is spinning and stable, it is called a gyroscope. The gyroscopic action of the spinning Twirl-o-Tube keeps it steady and stable in flight.

Super Twirl-o-Tube

An aluminum can makes a terrific Twirl-o-Tube, but it's more difficult to create. Ask an adult to help you when cutting the can.

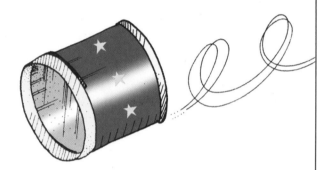

YOU WILL NEED

- an aluminum soft-drink can
- scissors that won't be ruined by cutting aluminum
- heavy tape such as masking tape
- an adult helper
- clear tape, a ruler

1 Have an adult use the point of the scissors to make a hole in the side of the can near one end. Cut all the way around the end of the can — be careful to avoid metal splinters.

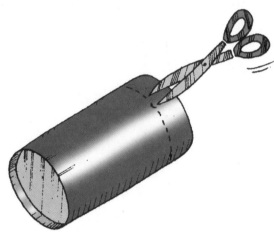

2 The cut end will have a few sharp points on it. Carefully cut them off. The can may also be bent. After you have removed the sharp bits, bend the can back into its original shape.

3 Measure the distance across the end of the can (the diameter). Cut off the other end of the can so that the length is the same as the diameter. This tube is 6.5 cm (2 ½ in.) in diameter, so it is cut 6.5 cm (2 ½ in.) long. Again, be sure to remove any sharp pieces.

6.5 cm (2 ½ in.)

6.5 cm (2 ½ in.)

4 Put a single layer of heavy tape at one end of the tube as shown. This is the front of your Super Twirl-o-Tube. On the other end put a single layer of clear tape. The end with the clear tape is the back.

Front

5 Follow steps 3 and 4 on page 29 for flying your Super Twirl-o-Tube.

Flying Meat Tray

Save the Styrofoam from under meat or vegetables and try making the incredible Flying Meat Tray (FMT).

1 Trim off the curved edges of the meat tray and cut the flat piece that remains into a square.

2 With a marker, draw a triangle on the Styrofoam as shown. Cut along the lines with scissors. You will use the big triangle as the FMT's wings and one of the small triangles as the fins and rudder.

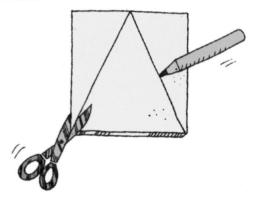

3 Cut a slot to the midpoint of the large triangle. The slot should be just wide enough so that another piece of Styrofoam will fit into it snugly.

Cut slot

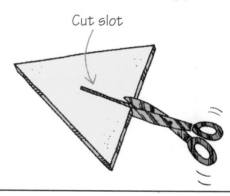

4 Cut a slot not quite to the midpoint of the rudder, as shown. This slot should be the same width as the one in step 3.

Cut slot

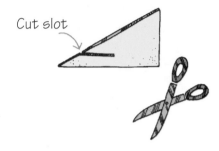

5 Cut off the front of the rudder at an angle as shown.

6 Push the rudder into the wing so that the two slots fit together.

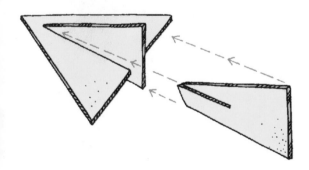

7 If the rudder is loose, tape it to the wing. When fitted in, the rudder should stick out a little past the end of the wing. Mark a fold line on the rudder as shown.

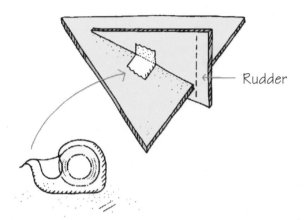

Rudder

8 Make a cut 1 cm (½ in.) long on each side of the rudder. Then make a fold line as shown. These flaps are your elevators.

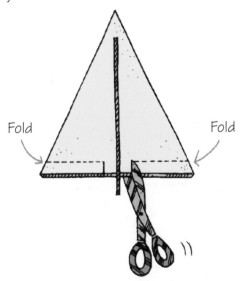

Fold

Fold

Finishing the FMT

When you first make it, the FMT is out of balance. Here's how to get it flying properly.

1 Use paper clips to add weight to the nose. For a small FMT, one or two paper clips will be enough. For a larger FMT, you may need more paper clips, or you may even have to tape on a coin.

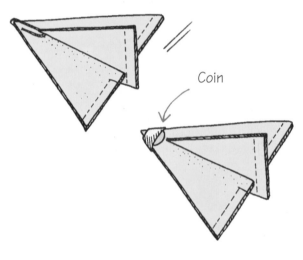

Coin

2 Straighten the rudder and bend the elevators up slightly.

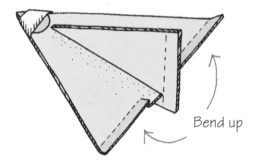

Bend up

3 Throw your FMT in a gentle glide. If it dives to the ground, try bending the elevators up more or removing some nose weight.

4 If the FMT glides slowly and falls in a series of swoops, try bending the elevators down a little or adding more nose weight. Keep adjusting the elevators and nose weight until you're satisfied with the glide.

FMT Aerobatics

THE LOOP
Throw the FMT straight ahead hard.

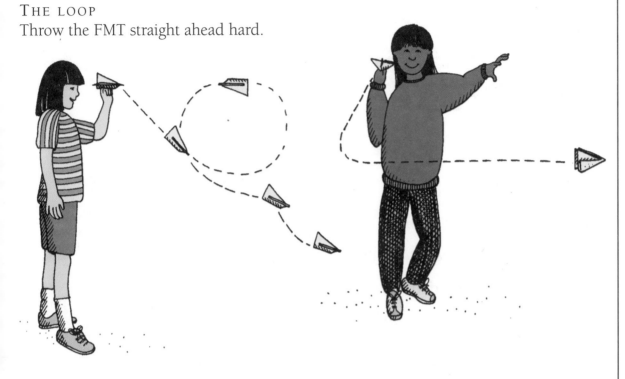

THE TURN
Bend the rudder slightly. Make sure
both elevators are bent equally.

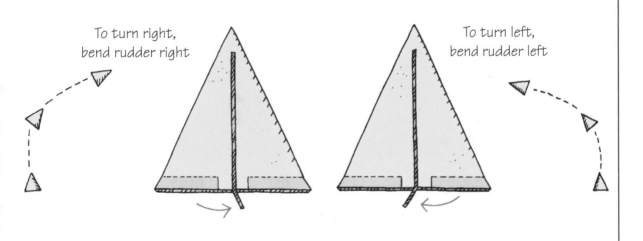

To turn right,
bend rudder right

To turn left,
bend rudder left

Chapter Four

PARACHUTES

Parachutes were first thought of long ago. In fact, parachutes were probably the first practical flying device. But for a long time, no one bothered making one. Why not? Until balloons and planes were invented, there wasn't really any need for them.

Tissue Chute

This small, light parachute is great for indoor flying. It's too delicate for outdoors.

YOU WILL NEED

- a Kleenex or other facial tissue
- thread
- a small paper clip or other small object to use as a weight
- scissors, a ruler

1 Cut your tissue so that it's square. Most tissues have two layers. If possible, separate the layers and use only one to make the Tissue Chute.

2 Cut four pieces of thread. Each piece should be twice as long as one side of the tissue. So if your tissue measures 19 cm (7 ½ in.) along one side, each string should be 38 cm (15 in.).

3 Tie one thread to each corner of the tissue as shown.

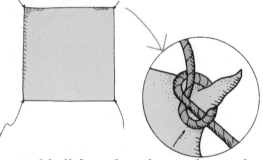

4 Hold all four threads together and let the tissue hang. Tie the four threads together in a knot about halfway between the tissue and the thread ends. Check that the threads are the same length from the knot to the tissue. If they aren't, try again. When they are the same length, tie another knot over the first one.

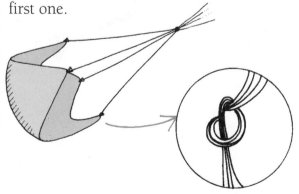

5 Tie the paper clip or other light weight to the thread below the knot.

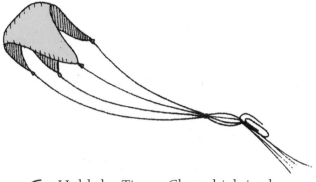

6 Hold the Tissue Chute high in the air by the top of the tissue. Check that the threads aren't tangled and let it drop.

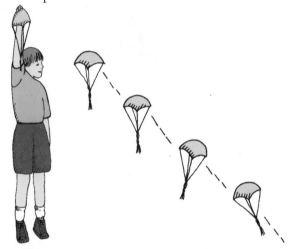

Flying Tips

If the Tissue Chute falls too fast, the weight is too heavy. Replace it with a lighter weight.

If it falls slowly but swings wildly from side to side, the weight is too light. Add a bit more weight. Keep experimenting until your Tissue Chute drops slowly and swings gently.

Heavy-duty Chute

To make a parachute suitable for outdoors, you need something larger and stronger than the Tissue Chute. The sky's the limit for long, high flights outdoors with this Heavy-duty Chute.

- a square cloth handkerchief or scarf (check with an adult first)
- light string
- a weight, such as a cork or keys
- scissors, a measuring tape or ruler

1 Follow steps 2 to 4 for the Tissue Chute on pages 36 to 37.

2 Tie a weight to the strings below the knot.

3 Hold the parachute by the center of the handkerchief and roll it up towards the weight. Keep folding the sides in so that the roll of cloth is neat.

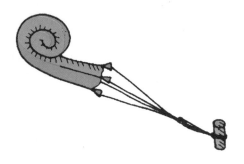

4 Wrap the strings around the roll of cloth. The weight must be on the outside or the strings will become tangled when the Heavy-duty Chute is thrown.

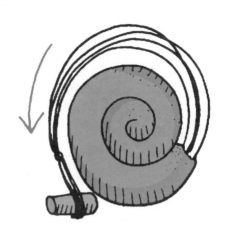

5 Throw the Heavy-duty Chute as high as possible into the air.

Flying Tips

If the Heavy-duty Chute falls too fast, try a lighter weight.

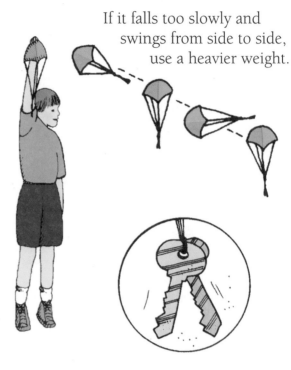

If it falls too slowly and swings from side to side, use a heavier weight.

Even with an ideal weight, your parachute will always swing slightly. Real parachutes often have a hole in the top of the handkerchief part to change the air flow and reduce the swinging.

On a real parachute, the handkerchief part is called a canopy and the strings are called shroud lines. There are many more shroud lines on a real chute.

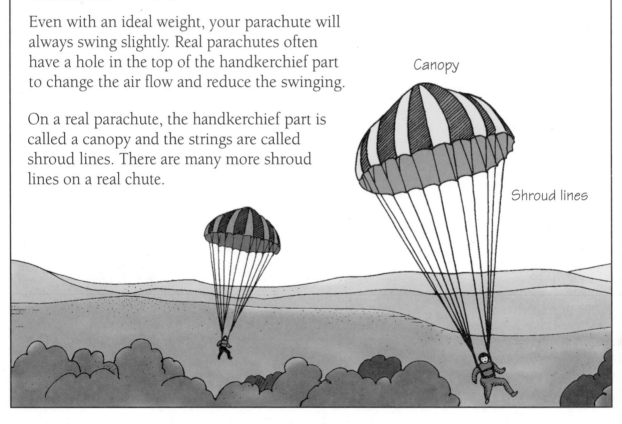

Canopy

Shroud lines